A
PRAYER
for Every Day

Translated from Dutch
by Peter Buma

A PRAYER FOR EVERY DAY

Published in 2013 by Peter Buma,
petebuma@gmail.com

ISBN-13: 978-1-940164-18-2

Printed by Color House Graphics, Grand Rapids, MI 2013.

Blessings!
Peter Buma

A
PRAYER
for Every Day

TRANSLATED FROM DUTCH
BY PETER BUMA

The front cover bears a picture taken by me of the stained glass window in the south balcony of the Eastern Avenue Christian Reformed Church, located along Eastern Avenue in Grand Rapids, Michigan.

I found this book, EEN BEDE VOOR ELKE DAG (A PRAYER FOR EVERY DAY) at the home of my mother after she passed away in the Netherlands. After reading a few pages I was impressed with the way in which this prayer book was written. We took the book home to

Michigan with us and after reading some more I became convinced that if I enjoyed reading it others would also like it and find it a blessing. And that is why I translated the book.

This prayer book was first written in German and then translated into Dutch by J. H. Gunning in 1935. It was very popular, and my copy is from the 20th edition which was printed in 1975.

Recently I was given permission by the publishers Thieme-Meulenhoff in the Netherlands to publish this in English.

It is my prayer that these prayers will be a blessing to you.

Peter Buma
Grand Rapids, Michigan 2013

Acknowledgements:

My thanks go to the following individuals for their encouragement and for their support in translating this prayer book:

Dr. Henry Baron for being the final editor

Amy Cole of Design Solutions for
the layout work

Sandy Gould and Color House Graphics
for printing

Ed Brouwer, my nephew in the
Netherlands, for getting permission to have
this prayer book printed from the publishers:
Thieme-Meulenhoff

My wife Milly for typing and early editing

My sincere thanks to all of you.

Table of Contents

January

I

My Father, may everything become new in me today! Make old duties new, make my love new, make my faith new. Grant me the desire for a new heaven and a new earth.

II

Eternal Father, I take my refuge in your grace. Let me not be without your protection in this world. Let me feel that a wall of fire is round about me. In your care I feel safe and comfortable.

III

Merciful Father, let me walk before you with respect. Let me feel your presence everywhere. Let me acknowledge in all things your providential love. Be with me wherever I go.

IV

Merciful Father, help me in the battle against temptation. Whenever I have difficulty, may the conqueror's banner of my Savior wave overhead. Make me a good soldier of Christ.

V

Father of all life, give me an overflowing love. Deliver me from all indecision. I pray that everything in me may praise your holy name. Give me the strength of eternal life.

VI

Savior of the world, I pray for everyone who labors, for the spreading of your Kingdom. Shower your blessings on all who witness to the poor and lost, the small and the great, the powerful and the weak, in this land and across the entire world.

VII

Father, make my heart wide and my love rich.
Make my life resemble that of a shady tree
so that tired walkers may find
rest and refreshment.

VIII

My Father, I pray for all the families of our
nation. May parents and children show the
world a true example of holy living.
Bless our love. Make our households
wells of living water.

IX

Heavenly Father, I thank you that all good
was given from your Fatherly hand. May I
joyfully come close to you, the living well,
from which I may draw in the name of Christ
my Savior. When I fall, let your overflowing
grace and indubitable promise of your
communion be with me.

X

My God, show me my most dangerous sin.
Help me recognize it when I see my temptation,
when I need to keep watch because I am
threatened. Qualify me for the good fight.
Make me strong through your grace.

XI

My Father, give that in this day a good
influence may go out from me. Let me not
become a hindrance to any seeking soul, but
give that all whom you send on my path,
through association with me, become better
and are driven closer to you.

XII

God of light, illuminate my spirit. Shine in all
the dark hiding places of my heart and make
me a child of the light. Discover my secret
sins and teach me to hate them. Renew my
desire. Give me a clean heart.

XIII

My Father, lead me on the road to life. Show me that the broad and easy road leads to slavery and that my coveting brings eternal sadness. Help me to recognize the good and to embrace it.

XIV

Heavenly Father, give me the assurance of your closeness. Let me live for you as I see you in the faces of those around me. May I never doubt your willingness. Confirm in me the unwavering assurance that with you the strength of everlasting life surrounds me.

XV

O my Father, all things are possible for those who believe. Lord, increase my faith. Let me peaceably overcome all difficulties. Strengthen me through your power for my life's journey. Let the mountain of burdens become for me a smooth road.

XVI

Holy Father, make my heart so wide that all my brothers and sisters can find a place there. Let me look not only at what is mine but also at what belongs to someone else. Deliver me from the bondage of self-interest.

XVII

O Christ, my King, make me obedient. Give that every thought is according to your will. Let my soul, without distraction and in deep reverence, serve you.

XVIII

My Savior, teach me also to pray for those I do not love. Take the blinders away from my eyes so that I may see the good in them. Show me how to love my enemies.

XIX

Almighty God, I thank you that you have called me to your community. Teach me to pray persistently, without stopping. Deliver me from the slavery of earthly thoughts which prevent my thinking about you. Grant me the freedom of heavenly joy.

XX

My Father, make me free in your service. So often I am prevented from fulfilling my duty as your child. Make my feet strong and fast. Help me willingly to do good things with joy.

XXI

God of all mercy, I lift my soul to you. Refresh
my soul and give me new life. Let me not
become sluggish in your service. Give that the
water of life will refresh and strengthen
me without interruption.

XXII

My Lord and my God, make me faithful
in the little things. Let the smallest details
in my life respect your holiness. Give that
I conscientiously fulfill your will. Lord,
strengthen my faith, and through
my faith, my obedience.

XXIII

Dear Father, grant me the assurance that
I am your pardoned child. Let me
always be close to you and let me know
that my sins are forgiven.

XXIV

My Father, let the waters of life on this day
be richly poured out over all your people.
Refresh the troubled. Soften the hardened
hearts. Let the wilderness bear fruit again.
Awaken the dead to life.

XXV

Almighty God, I pray for all who struggle and
are so helpless. Help them believe that you
will not leave them. Show them how much
Christ does for them and let them gain the
royal victory through Him who loves them to
the uttermost.

XXVI

My Father, awake in me the spirit of
thankfulness. Let me not accept your grace as
if I had earned it. Let me praise you every day
anew for your free grace and mercy.

XXVII

Great God, I pray for my country. Bless our president and our government. Let the dew of your grace refresh and strengthen. Bind us more closely to you and to our country.

XXVIII

My Father, help me to better understand the goal of my life here on earth. May I not misuse my days. Do not my days belong to you? Show me the immense worth of time. Let me so live that every day and every hour glorify your name.

XXIX

My Savior, let me here upon the earth with all its instability inhale the air of eternity. Let the strong winds of God's high mountains continually lift me up and give me new strength.

XXX

Merciful God, teach me to understand your gentle meekness. Make me to know that it is the well-spring of true power. Let my strength come to help those who are weak. Let it be an honor that I may share my brothers' and sisters' burdens.

XXXI

My Father, I thank you for my daily bread. Grant that I may ever enjoy it with reverence and gratitude. Nourish me with the bread of life. Let me grow in grace and in sanctification. Keep me ever close to Jesus.

February

I

My Lord, you have allowed me through your grace to begin a new month. Give that I may both begin and end this month with you. Help me to keep your commandments and to find joy in them.

II

Almighty God, let it be that your will is also mine. Let me not desire anything other than you. Let all false joys become bitter. Give that I long only for that which is holy and good; be a joy to me.

III

My Father, let me see my sins in the light of your face and not in the shadow of human judgment. In the light I see your brightness. Place my sins in that light so that I will be afraid and hate them.

IV

My Father. grant access to your rich goods in
all my need. Let your stars shine in my night,
make clear to me what I should be doing.
Send your angels to comfort me in my trials.

V

My Savior, help me in all things to think
about your holy example. Give that the words
I speak may be spoken in love with holy
friendliness. Pour out your Holy Spirit,
O Jesus Christ.

VI

My Lord and my God, I will honor and
serve you. May I not long for anything
that is contrary to your will. Deliver me
from self-seeking and raise me up to
a life in the light.

VII

Holy Father, give that I may hold fast my inheritance in Jesus Christ. Let me take part in the riches of my Savior. May I be clothed in righteousness. Put shoes on my feet so that I may serve the gospel of peace.

VIII

My Father, if at the beginning of this day some unclean thoughts are in my heart, take them away from me! When I desire something that would offend my brother or sister, may it die in me through your grace.

IX

My God, I thank you for this new day and for all the grace you give me today. Let it not be an unproductive day for me. Help me understand what it is you want to teach me. Give that the harvest of this day will endure until tomorrow.

X

Merciful Lord, may it not be a hollow
sound when I say I am a disciple of yours.
Give that my brothers and sisters may
notice when you make me genuinely
kind and cause me to show concern.
Bless me so that others may know that
I belong to you.

XI

My Father, what is it that you have to tell me
today? Grant that I may understand it clearly.
Give me a listening ear and an attentive
heart. Give that I may recognize truth in the
midst of so much untruth. May I discern and
faithfully love your Gospel.

XII

Heavenly Father, make my soul healthy. Let it
not be poisoned by the contamination of
the world. Protect me from the inclinations to
evil which may come over me. Heal me
Lord, then I shall be truly healed.

XIII

Heavenly Father, make me rich in the
knowledge of your truth. Give me every day
new strength from your Holy Word. Protect
me from unworthy thoughts which harm me
inwardly and make the labor of my life
worthless. Grant me the mind of Christ.

XIV

My Father, I thank you for all the blessings of
this life. Help me to see and count them
for I long for my life to become an
uninterrupted song of praise.

XV

O God, my Father, deliver me from the unrest of this world and fill my heart with constant love and reverence for you. Do not allow adverse thoughts to tear me apart. Let me feel hunger and thirst for you and you alone.

XVI

Almighty God, your Word is my guide. I will hold fast to it, also when it becomes difficult to be obedient to it and to abide by it. Help me to walk the right path even when it becomes difficult, as it did for you with thorns. Your will be done.

XVII

My Father, teach me to pray without stopping. Make my communion with you continue undisturbed. Help me to stay focused on you. Let me live under the shadow of your wings.

XVIII

Great God, give me a gentle spirit. Let me
with soft but strong hands treat the wounds
of the world. Protect me from godlessness
and from loveless judgment.

XIX

Holy Spirit, keep my remembrances fresh so
that I may think on your blessings. Allow me
never to forget my sins and keep me humble.
May I always think of your mercies and place
my hope in you. Give that I may continually
lift my eyes to the mountains.

XX

My Father, let your Holy Spirit be present
and working in me today. Make every day a
Sabbath in unbroken consecration.
Let all labor be to your praise and glory.

XXI

Almighty God, let the rays of your
goodness ignite my heart. Spare me from
lukewarmness and indifference. Help me to
abide in you. Baptize me with the
Holy Spirit and with fire.

XXII

Merciful God, I lift my eyes full of faith and
expectation to you. Let me walk with you
today in new and perfect communion. Your
word is my light and your grace my strength.
In the power of your love will I love my
brothers and sisters.

XXIII

My Father, in your will I find happiness. I will
not just follow you but I will do so with joy.
Your law is my delight and your will
my true happiness.

XXIV

My Father in heaven, bind me through a strong and holy bond with my brothers and sisters. Spare me from discord and from all that might lead to alienation. Give that my thoughts and words may serve for the peace of your children.

XXV

Lord my God, make me sure of your forgiveness. Help me now that you have forgiven my sins, that I may wholeheartedly hate them, and cause me to want nothing to do with them.

XXVI

Heavenly Father, let your grace rest upon me. May I experience some of your power today. Deliver me from loneliness and self-seeking. Help me to abide in your loving communion.

XXVII

Heavenly Father, your mercy is seen in all the works of your hands. May they also be seen in me. Help me to know your wonderful mercy, you who take care of my life. Teach me to understand that I live from day to day out of your goodness.

XXVIII

Holy Father, let your bright light also shine today in my soul. Let the glory of your gospel become greater for me so that I may give my heart to that gospel. Feed me with the bread of life.

XXIX

My Father, may I also work for your Kingdom. Prevent me from working against you. Make me truly a servant of Jesus Christ.

March

I

Merciful Lord, I praise and thank you that you are giving an everlasting value to the daily work of this wretched creature of yours. Let the results of my labor be improved through the hope of your coming again.

II

O Father of all living, strengthen the communion of your children. Join their hearts and may they become one in the knowledge of and gratitude for the Savior they share.

III

My Lord, forgive all that I have done in which I have failed, and bless that which was according to your will. Help me that I may remain true to you, and let my ending be better than my beginning so that it becomes light when eventide arrives.

IV

My God, when I become restless, help me to
abide in the shadow of the Almighty. Make
me calm and peaceable in the battle and
in the temptations.

V

My Lord and my Savior, help me to stay
close so that I follow you in this day. Give
that I do not fear the cross but that I
willingly carry it when you place it upon me.
Give that I may willingly lose my life so that
I may gain it in truth.

VI

Merciful Lord, I thank you for all that makes
this life lovely. How my undeserved blessings
have been placed in my path! I thank you for
the kindness of others, for all people who
are filled with love and compassion, for love
shown to an autistic student by his classmates.

VII

Heavenly Father, may I feel your presence.
Make your presence known and may I feel it
as if it were an earthly friend who is with me.
Grant me the sweetness of your communion,
and may I never lose it.

VIII

Loving Lord, spare your people the fear of
enslavement. Let my life not be torn apart by
unbelief. Protect me so that the calamities
and worries will not drive me to despair.
Help me to trust in you.

IX

O Lord my God, make me to be a branch of
the true vine. Cause me to give all the praise
to you that I may bear much fruit. Let the
people see my good works and let the poor
and disconsolate receive courage and
comfort from me.

X

Almighty Lord, I wish to begin my day's work with you. Support my weakness with your power and make me strong so that I may carry out your will with joy.

XI

My Father, guide my life today. Protect the gates of my mind. Control my seeing and hearing. Bring my thoughts under your control. Bend my ear so that I may understand your Word.

XII

O Lord my God, grant me blessed assurance that I through my Savior have been reconciled to you. Let me as a child stay in the home of my Father. Take me in your holy communion and let me take part in the rich gifts of your table.

XIII

Father, let my work serve you. Bless and purify my work of today so that it may be a blessing to my soul.

XIV

My Savior, make me to be soft-hearted and submissive. Grant me a quiet spirit. Deliver me from inner turmoil and instability. Grant me your peace.

XV

Spirit of love, encourage everyone who has important responsibilities in my country. Shed your light on those who through speech and writing speak to others so that clear and holy power may go out from them.

XVI

Merciful God, show me how I can ease the
grief of the world. Help me today to ease the
burdens and lighten the afflictions of my
fellow citizens as I see them cross my path.
Fill me with your compassion so that I may
comfort and refresh the wounded
and brokenhearted.

XVII

My Father, I would so willingly give everything
to you. Make my thoughts pure and my
feelings sensitive, and bless my will, O Lord.

XVIII

Heavenly Father, shape my heart by your
will so that I may fear your name. Bring
everything that is contrary to you to
obedience so that no discordant sound
disturbs the full harmony but everything in
me praises and loves your holy name.

XIX

Everlasting God, let my winter become
spring. Whatever is cold and frozen in me,
cause it to thaw and melt through the glow of
your grace. Let me live for you and bear fruit.

XX

Holy Spirit, grant that I will more and more
give myself as a complete offering. Let your
boundless and unlimited grace work in me.
May your Kingdom come to me and
through me to others.

XXI

My Savior, make me live as a child of
the light. Keep me from grumbling and
complaining. Let me never become a child
of the night with a heavy heart. Fill me with
the hope of happiness and cause others to be
assured and gain strength through me.

XXII

O peace-loving King, make an end to the strife among the people. Take away all the trivial things that bother us. Deliver us from all bitterness and make us free from all mistrust and suspicion.

XXIII

My Father, show me your brightness to the extent that my eyes can take it in. Reveal to my soul something of your beauty and bring me to a deeper worship and complete surrender.

XXIV

Almighty God, whenever you wish you can clean me. Help me believe that you can grant me cleansing. Give me the assurance that through the power of Jesus the pollution of the world can be taken away. Create in me, O Lord, a clean heart and renew in me a steady Spirit.

XXV

God of Love, teach me to carry my cross.
Grant that I do not try to shake it from me,
that I do not choose the easy road of my own
pleasure, but the road of duty even if this is
the bearing of my cross.

XXVI

Everlasting God, let everything that I start be
blessed by you. Renew my spirit so that I in
heavenly conviction may perform my earthly
work. Give me the wisdom and power
to strive for that which is from above.

XXVII

Father of all people, hear me when I pray for
my brothers and sisters in this world. Let the
light of the cross go before their eyes and
hearts so that their yoke becomes easy and
their burden light.

XXVIII

Holy Father. let your bright light also shine
today in my soul. Let the glory of your
Gospel become greater for me so that I may
give my heart to that Gospel. Feed me
with the bread of life.

XXIX

My Father may I also work for your Kingdom.
Prevent me from working against you.
Make me truly a servant of Jesus Christ.

XXX

Eternal God, you have carried me through with
so much patience, may I have patience toward
others. Show me the blessing of humility while
carrying the burden of others.Do not allow me
to disturb your will with my thoughts. Help me
to rest in you and to wait for you.

XXXI

Merciful Savior, gather the poor pieces of my life and make something good in your eyes. Forgive my unbelief. Forgive me for everything that I should have done but did not do. Let your goodness and mercy support me.

April

I

Heavenly Father, open my eyes to the wonders of your goodness. Your benevolence and the riches of your grace have become so ordinary for me. Give that I may see the wonder so that I may love and praise you and enjoy you every day.

II

Merciful God, I believe that you are God Almighty. Help me that my belief may not only be words but your truth. Grant that in everything I do I will be subjected and obedient to no other will but yours. Your will alone be done.

III

Risen Lord and Savior, let me today think upon your death on the cross. Lord, let me bear your death in my body.

IV

Merciful God, in your mercy enclose my polluted and lost life in your generous forgiveness. Deliver me from the power of sin. Set me free from debt and grant me your blessed peace.

V

Merciful Father, grant me the spirit of meekness. Deliver me from hardness and pride. Help me to use my power to help my brothers and sisters carry their cross.

VI

My Savior, make me conform to your death so that I may experience the power of your resurrection. Lift me out of my death to a new life. Let today become for me a beautiful Easter Day.

VII

Heavenly Father, grant me in your mercy all
that I am in need of. Let me not hesitate and
be afraid of tomorrow but help me so that I
today in faithful obedience may serve you. Let
my life show that Christ truly lives in me.

VIII

My Savior, you have known the difficulty and
the labor of life here upon earth. Bless my
labor so that it may prosper. Protect me from
all falsehood so that I may truly serve you.

IX

Heavenly Father, help me not to lose
my heavenly inheritance and remain
outside of your communion which you
have opened to me. Let me find in you my
heavenly home. Grant me the joy and
freedom of your children.

X

Lord Jesus, my Savior, let me today arise from
the grave of sin. Make my walk with you a
walk in heaven. Lift me into the life above.
Let me see your beauty.

XI

Eternal God, God of hope. Let some of your
light fall on me and deliver me from the
enslavement of fear and doubt. Let me know
you and the light of life.

XII

O my Savior, in the early morning I lift my
song to you. Let me in joyful obedience
always be filled with a love song. Let no
negative thoughts and unkindness hinder
those who follow you. In you, O Lord,
I will seek happiness.

XIII

Risen Lord and Savior, let me grow in your grace and knowledge. May I understand ever more perfectly the mystery of your life and death. Let me rise to a new life with you.

XIV

My Savior, I praise you for obtaining life eternal. I thank you that you took away the curtain. Let me walk as I should as a child of the everlasting God. Make me worthy to be called your child.

XV

Heavenly Father, make me sure of my kinship and let it be so beautiful and lovely to me that I may worthily fulfill your call and never willfully turn to sin. Grant that I will live as a child of the King and that nothing negative may be found in me.

XVI

Eternal Father, let me hear your voice today.
Grant that all the shouting of the world will
not mute the heavenly voice. Help me that I will
not only hear your voice in my inner chamber
but also amidst the clamor of the people.

XVII

My risen Lord, let me experience the power of
the resurrection. Raise me above the turmoil
of the world. Raise me up to a heavenly life so
that I may be a blessing to others.

XVIII

My Father, let me obey you willingly today.
Let my duty be my happiness and your
commandments my joy.

XIX

Heavenly Father, make me a child of hope.
Do not let my soul be pulled down by fear
and unbelief. Let me trustingly wait for the
morning when I live in the dark valley. Grant
that the people I know may see that I am
a friend of Christ.

XX

Merciful God, ignite in me the fire of holy
love. Do not let the spirit of this world
extinguish it. Let it glow brightly in spite
of all hindrances. Help me until my
dying days to be faithful.

XXI

Holy Father, let me find rest in you. I want so
much to be free from all the hustle and bustle
and find peace in you. Deliver me from all
that stands in the way, from all wrong desires
and unnecessary worries.

XXII

Holy God, I offer my body to you. Let me never forget that it is a temple of the Holy Spirit. Help me to live a life of order and wisdom. May I understand that the laws of health are commandments of God.

XXIII

God of power, make me ready for the battle of this day. Let me not falter with the first encounter. Grant that I am victorious over every temptation. Let me be more than a conqueror through Christ.

XXIV

Heavenly Father, bend down to your people. Let your people see your beauty, to know the truth when surrounded by lies. Show mercy to those who want to know you. Stir in them the longing for holiness and direct their feet on the road to peace.

XXV

My Father, make me truly to love my neighbor. Deliver me from the slavery of self-seeking. Grant me the freedom to love. Enlarge my heart so that I may serve you and my neighbor.

XXVI

Holy Father, teach me to hate my sin. Direct my thoughts to what is good and pure. Always show me more of your wonderful glory and make me conform to your image.

XXVII

Holy Spirit, illumine my meditations and deliver me from impure thoughts so that I may understand what is good and what is evil. In your light I see light.
Let me walk in that light.

XXVIII

My Father in heaven, let me see from afar
the throne of light. Let my life be filled with
reverence. Let me walk as one who knows
the glory of heaven, and do not allow me to
spend my years in vanity.

XXIX

Lord my God, the work of this day begins
again. Give me pure thoughts in all that I do,
bless me, Lord, and let me feel your closeness.

XXX

Merciful Father, do not let this month come
to an end without my experience of
closeness with you. Forgive me for my
disobedience, forgive my hypocrisy. Wash me
clean through your grace and let me begin a
new time period with a pure heart.

May

I

O God, lift me to the light on high.
Do not let me stumble around in the dark.
Illumine my heart and my spirit
with your joyful grace. Ignite my words,
thoughts and work so that the people may
see that I am a child of the light. Deliver me
from the slavery of darkness.

II

Heavenly Father, I thank you that
you take care of me. Your mercy is
endless. You crown the day with your
goodness. Help me to recognize all your
blessings. Deliver me from my spiritual
blindness. Show me your footprints
all over creation.

III

Holy God, let the beauty of spring
stir my heart to praise and thankfulness,
you my Creator and Re-Creator: Break the
power of winter in me. Grant me your
spirit so that he may drive away frost and
cold, and the joy of the Lord may find
room to come in.

IV

My Father in heaven, show me the
importance of the little things. Help me
to honor and hold holy these little things.
Teach me in every moment of this day
to bring the light of your presence
so that, O Father, my entire life's
journey belongs to you.

V

Merciful God, through your grace make my spirit open and compassionate. Deliver me from the superficiality of the love of this world which is full of ingratitude and pride. Grant me the spirit of Christ.

VI

O God, my Father, help me to walk the road of life with a steady pace. Lift up your tired child again and strengthen the stumbling feet so that I enter the battle to spread your mercy courageously for my King.

VII

Heavenly Father, grant me the grace so that through my life brotherly and sisterly love may increase among the people. Keep me from increasing the chasms among your children. Help me to plant and strengthen friendship and trust.

VIII

My loving Lord, support me so that I
may encounter all that is difficult and
uncomfortable with calmness and strength.
Grant that my disappointments will
become blessings.

IX

My Father, help me today to exercise a good
and kindly influence. Help me through my
steady faith to refresh the fearful and to
restore the disheartened. May I through my
inner joy make others happy.

X

My Father, let me not be forgotten in
my grief. Do not forsake me but stand beside
me. You know what I need and how
much I can bear.

XI

Eternal Father, your blessing is my happiness and in your peace I find rest. Therefore I pray, be merciful to me. Grant me to be a part of your Godly gifts. Guide me to take from your Word strength for the work of this day.

XII

My Father, teach me to distinguish the eternal from that which does not last. Grant that I may discover your Spirit in the reading of your Word.

XIII

Almighty God, shine on me the light of your face. Let the love of my God make my heart happy. Let me not long for earthly glory but let me please my King. Your will be done.

XIV

Father of light, I thank you for every person who gives me admonition and warns me, who through spoken or written word increases my knowledge. For all that makes my life richer, I give you praise and honor.

XV

Father of all mercy, I thank you for my daily bread. Grant that I may take it from you as a gift and not as if I had a right to it. Let it be for me a sign of your grace and cause me to enjoy it in humility and gratitude.

XVI

My Father, I bring my sins before your face. Destroy their power over my soul and stamp all that I have done wrong out of your holy book for Jesus sake.

XVII

Merciful God, I pray for all young Christians.
Strengthen them in their difficulties. Take
away their fear of the power of the tempter.
Let their inner life ripen in the
light of your grace.

XVIII

Holy Spirit, live in me. Lead me in your truth.
Let me gaze upon your everlasting beauty.
Let the commandments of the Lord be my
joy. Make me a true disciple of Jesus Christ.

XIX

O Lord, grant me a lively and peaceful
consciousness that I am your child.
Help me to think seriously about my calling
so that I avoid doing foolish things.
Do not let my feet slip.

XX

Merciful God, let me also today be a child of the light. Help me so that I may remain in communion with you. Help me to understand how great my inheritance is in Christ, and let me walk in the wedding robes of your Kingdom.

XXI

Merciful Spirit, form my soul and make me spiritually dependent upon you. Help me to discern the movements of your wings and may I also hear your gently calling voice

XXII

Savior of the world, I pray for all who proclaim your Word. Strengthen them richly through your grace so that their proclamation may be filled with your strength. Let them see your beauty so that they may fulfill their calling with joy. Grant that the world will accept their witness.

XXIII

My Father, show me how I may truly serve you. Prevent me from selfishly cutting myself off from others. Show me the joy of getting to know those who happily in self-denial and honesty seek the good of my fellow believers.

XXIV

Holy Spirit, let my communion with you become more earnest. Do not allow me to just be satisfied with the truth but grant that I have a burning love to hunger and thirst after your righteousness and presence.

XXV

My Father, let the glorious light of your gospel enter my soul so that the heavenly seed will sprout in me and the buds of all that is good and pure may be shown in all of their beauty.

XXVI

Holy Father, I dedicate the labor of this day to you. Place the seal of Christ on it and take away my pride in self so that I may in my daily profession not be a hindrance to my fellow believers.

XXVII

My Father, deliver me from all fear which saps my strength. Help me to fear only sin while powerfully and courageously defending the truth.

XXVIII

My Father, may I walk today as a true child of yours. Let the sureness of my kinship fill me with holy respect, and may I be worthy of my high calling.

XXIX

My God, I pray for your Kingdom. Grant that
I may love your Kingdom in earnest and
obediently defend it. Let your power be made
known to me in order that I may happily be
your witness. Let me taste the love of your
Kingdom so that I also may speak to
others about your glory.

XXX

My Father, let me expect great things today.
Make me go through life with purpose. Help
me to keep my eyes open and wait for you,
my Lord. Help me to see you in everything
that is lovely and clean.
Help me to love your appearance.

XXXI

Holy Spirit, you have gifts for the children of the people. You have the gift of peace, happiness, and rest. I come to you in my poverty, without money, and without power in myself. Grant me your treasure in grace and give me eternal riches.

June

I

Great God, let this be a month of rich inner growth for me. Make me heavenly minded. Grant that I may never stoop to that which is mean or unclean. Make me in your power to seek that which is above.

II

Holy Spirit, let me feel your presence. Let it be not in beautiful words but in holy reality for me. I want to find my happiness in you and there to rejoice in your power. Let me see everything in your light.

III

Heavenly Father, make me faithful in my prayer life. Grant that I may feel the suffering of the persecuted and those who sorrow. Let me give thanks with those who rejoice. Let me fight for the souls of the people and plead on their behalf before the throne of grace.

IV

Holy Spirit, bless my whole life. Grant that my daily work will be a prayer so that through it I will become ever purer and better. May I hunger and thirst for what is true.

V

Lord Jesus, all power resides in you. Help me to cut myself loose from this world and direct myself toward eternity. Let my walk with you, O Savior, become in me a reality.

VI

Heavenly Father, make my soul be as the budding garden. Spare me from drought and unfruitfulness. Grant that I will never be seen as poor, pitiful, and repulsive to others. May I as a Christian blossom in you and produce fruit.

VII

My Father, grant that this day may bring
me gain for eternity, a new view of my
obligations, a new assurance that I am a child
of the Most high.

VIII

Heavenly Father, I thank you for your love that
never ends. Help me to believe that your love
carries, undergirds, and gives me strength for
my task. I thank you for your faithfulness. Fill
me more and more with self-denial so that I
may give myself over to your holy will.

VIX

Holy Spirit, I thank you for the shining light
of this morning. O, could it be a pure image
of my soul. Let the light of eternity pierce my
heart. Then I can be happy and proclaim the
love of my God.

X

My Father, teach me to do your will. Prevent
me from corrupting your intentions. Make
me to be lovable in my words so that others
may be drawn to you.

XI

Holy Father, let me in quiet reverence live for
you. Grant that also my merry times will be
filled with holy fear, that also then I will
demonstrate that I am your child. Make me
open to having Christ live in me.

XII

Strong and mighty God, let the feeling of
your power be stronger in me than the feeling
of my weakness. Let me not go against my
enemies alone in my impotence but equip me
through your beautiful grace. Let me,
through Christ, become a conqueror.

XIII

God of love, stay next to me in the dark hours of my life. Let the hours be my friends and not my enemies. Grant that pain and adversity will make me richer in the things of heaven. Grant that temporary sadness will make me ready for your everlasting glory.

XIV

Merciful God, help me today to abide in you. Let all my power be rooted in you. Let everything that I do be like a stream of your Godly mercy that flows, and may my words be penetrated by your Spirit.

XV

My Father, teach me to accept your Spirit and truth. Grant that I with sensitivity will come to you. Make my life bear fruit to your praise.

XVI

Merciful God, let me walk with you today,
and let me do this in holy readiness for you
and your service. Grant me the festive
garments. Let my words be purified in the
holy fire of your Spirit. Make me worthy to be
called your friend.

XVII

Merciful Lord, show me my hidden faults.
Deliver me from my sins when I do not pay
attention. May my words be true to you.
Wash me clean of all injustice.
May I be true to myself.

XVIII

My Savior, let me today stay in living fellowship
with you. Let me know your secret and reveal
to me the hidden treasures of your glory. Grant
me a clean heart so that I may see God.

XIX

Merciful Lord, let me always love that which is good and noble. Take away the scales from my eyes and let me see things as you see them. Grant me the mind of Christ.

XX

Almighty God, make me strong through your peace. Deliver me from all unrest and worry. Let all my energy be directed to doing your will; then I will, without stopping, bring forth good fruit.

XXI

My Father, grant that I grow up in your knowledge through Jesus Christ. Let me see your glory in my daily work. Grant me always to feel a need for your indwelling grace.

XXII

Heavenly Father, grant me your grace so that I may hate all sin. You know how often I still have a secret longing for my sins. Grant me a new spirit so that I may truly flee from them.

XXIII

Holy Father, bless me so that I may become a blessing to others. Let there flow from me streams of living water. Help me to bring true happiness to those who have difficulty in their lives.

XXIV

Everlasting God, I thank you that you have made this earth so clean. I praise you because everything around me proclaims your majesty. Open my eyes that I may see the beauty of God. Grant to my soul the spirit of worship so that all the beauty of the world will lead me to you.

XXV

My Father, grant that I do not succumb to the things of the world but help me through your grace to work in making the world new in your image.

XXVI

Great God, teach me how I should walk in holy fear. Spare me from idle talk, flightiness, and other things that stand in the way when I pray to you, but let me always bow before you in the Spirit. Let me see your throne from afar.

XXVII

My Lord and my God, help me so that this day may have a good beginning and a good ending. Knit together the broken threads of holy intentions so that I my finish this day in complete surrender to you.

XXVIII

My Father, may your Spirit lead me in every hour of this day in order that my thoughts be illumined, my heart ignited, and that I may learn what to think and speak. Help me so that I do not grieve your Spirit in word or in deed.

XXIX

Almighty God, lead me to your council. Protect and lead me so that I do not make foolish decisions which could spoil my life. Let me look at you and grant me the mind of Christ. Teach me to know you and to follow you.

XXX

My Savior, let your Holy Spirit penetrate me today and through his work of grace make my soul healthy. Help me to live in the fear of the Lord.

July

I

Merciful God, I lift my heart up to you. May it remain today at the height of communion with you. May my thoughts not wander to unworthy things. Grant that my walk will be in heaven. May it be that your mercy governs my will.

II

Everlasting Father, source of light and peace, grant to me and to all those who pray to you today your blessed rest. Change our doubt into trust, our fear into peace, and our unrest into joy in your blessed communion.

III

Heavenly Father, may I keep my eye focused on you, also in my labor for daily bread. Spare me from running after that which does not last. Let me not seek my crown in material things but honestly strive toward that which is above.

IV

Merciful Lord, lead me in all truth. Spare me
from all self-seeking and unspiritual pride.
Open my heart to your truth. Grant that I will
find love in your light from above.

V

Merciful God, make me show mercy as you
are merciful. Open my heart and make me
have pity and love where there is sorrow and
pain. Grant that I may give comfort and
strength to your suffering children.

VI

My God, I offer you my life with all of its
shortcomings and stains. Have mercy on me.
Deliver me from all sadness and grant that
I will turn to you and be led to surrender
to your holy will.

VII

Heavenly Father, how wonderful are your
works in all the earth! You make the grass
grow on the mountains and fill the valleys
with flowers. The earth is full of your
goodness. Let your beauty stand before my
eyes so that I awaken with your lovely
image before me.

VIII

Almighty God, fountain of all blessing, draw
my heart in mercy to you on high. Let me
be as one with you in the depth of my soul.

IX

Father of all mercy, send your Spirit
to be among us. Let all authority and
government be in subjection to you. Bless our
government. Let all to whom you have given
power work toward that which is good and
pleasing to you.

X

My Father, help me to love and praise you.
Let me know your benefits and let the tone
of holy joy resound more and more in my
soul. Also put a new song in my mouth today.

XI

Holy Spirit, remember me above all in what I
so easily forget. Sanctify my memory so that
it will hold fast to that which is good and not
lose any of its treasures. Grant that I do not
have to relearn today what I learned yesterday.

XII

My Father, grant me the strong hope of a
life that has conquered. May I also when I
commit faults not throw up my hands in
despair. Strengthen my belief so that some day
I may awaken in your presence. Let me create
new enthusiasm through the riches of your
promises so that I may nevermore have fear.

XIII

My Father, let your heaven always be open
for me. Grant me a broad vision of your
splendor. Help me that again and again I may
see heaven and long after it. Let heaven
be my food and drink every day.

XIV

My Father, make me be as one of your
faithful disciples so that I will not depart
from you when I am tested. Grant that I may
willingly carry my cross and not choose the
broad road. Let me be crucified with you.

XV

My Father, let the end of my road be more
beautiful than the beginning. Let it be for me
the evening light. Let your forgiving love
drive away all of my clouds. Today may I
renew my covenant with you.

XVI

O God my loving Father, help me to do your
will. Let me see all things in your light.
Cut me loose from the works of darkness.
Grant me your Godly life so that I may
serve your people.

XVII

God, the only light, let your light shine in my
spirit. Stay by me when it becomes dark
for me; when my strength gives way, make
your Spirit stay with me so that I will live and
walk as a child of the light.

XVIII

My Father, teach me to be thankful. Show me
the riches of your grace so that without
stopping I may praise and love you. Deliver
me from the spirit of discontentment.

XIX

My Father, let me not forget that I belong
to one big family. Grant that through my
life its members become happier.
Grant that no one through my unfaithfulness
will experience discomfort and unhappiness,
that not one of them goes through life in
want because I have not done my duty.
Help me to help others.

XX

Everlasting God, let me experience
something of life eternal. Grant that the
hope of your glory will strengthen me in
perseverance and patience so that I will not
tire as I keep the goal in front of me.

XXI

My Father, may I believe in the world I have
not seen. When I am frightened by earthly
life and the life of the future seems so unsure,
reveal to me your conquering power.
Let me feel assured in you.

XXII

Heavenly Father, incline my heart that I may
keep your commandments. Deliver me
from all yearning toward evil, of everything
that darkens my vision. Make me truly
righteous and entirely clean where no other
eye sees me except yours.

XXIII

God of all power, look in tender mercy on my
weakness. Let me not be taken in by the
evil one but may I trust in your great power.
Make me invincible through your grace.

XXIV

Merciful God, I thank you for your Word. Grant that I may become an owner of its treasure. Let your promises strengthen my faith so that I walk the journey that has been given to me with patience and obedience, always looking upwards to Jesus.

XXV

My Father, make me focus on heaven. Help me to stay in communion with Christ. Let me look at his glory. Grant that his beauty may overcome and conquer my heart.

XXVI

Merciful Father, help me to believe that I in my weakness may do great things in Christ. Let me not be overwhelmed by earthly things but make me a child of the great promise. Let me ever come closer to the great goal of my life.

XXVII

My Father, let my thanks be new every morning. Let me acknowledge your grace better, so that my song of thanks may never stop. Make me a singing child of yours.

XXVIII

My Father, I long for the water of life. Grant that it today may become evident in my body as a fresh stream, so that it may clean me of all my sins, to strengthen what is good in me and renew what seems to be dying in my life. Make me a flowering garden.

XXIX

O Lord, help me today to rest in you. May I not become impatient. Grant that I, still and comforted, wait for your works until the clouds begin to move and I may follow you.

XXX

Merciful God, I pray for all whose lives
are not rich because of disappointments
and may never taste the sweetness of
earthly blessings. Be merciful to them and
spare them from feeling bitter. Let your
communion be a measureless and rich
compensation for them.

XXXI

My Father, make me sure of your
total forgiveness. Let the sins of yesterday not
threaten me again today. Wash me clean of all
debt and help me to hate my sins.
Let me stand before you in the white
garment of your justice.

August

I

O Lord my God, may I discover the beat of your presence. Let my soul understand the quiet wink and hear the heavenly calling. Grant that I in the busyness of the world may listen to the chimes of eternity.

II

Merciful God, grant me your gentleness. Fill me with happiness and love. Let violence and complaints be far from my soul. Grant that my heart may bring forth the fruit of the Spirit in honor of your holy name.

III

My Father, grant that I may find happiness in the beauty of the summer. Let its beauty awaken me to the longing for holy living. Cause me to bring forth flowers and fruits of the Spirit.

IV

My Father, let me not be vanquished. Do not allow prosperity to become a poison for my soul or disappointment make me bitter. Let all things serve me to the good and to your honor.

V

My Father in heaven, be my refuge in the midst of my enemy. Give that I may stand firm in the hour of temptation and will have no fear when danger is upon me. Grant me peace as guarantee that I belong to you.

VI

Heavenly Father, help me today to do something for you even if it is small. Let my work be a blessing for others. Let everything that I speak and do be filled with your Spirit. May I be an image bearer of my Lord.

VII

My Father, help me to pay attention to the
voice of the Master when he calls me to a
task, be it pleasant or unpleasant.

VIII

My God and Father, let the work of this day
be consecrated to you. I confess to you with
shame that my daily walk so often disgraces
my confession. Give me your Spirit
that my labor may be a blessing, and I will
become an instrument of your grace.

VIX

O Holy Spirit, penetrate my soul with
heaven's air. Let the evil in me die so that
the good may grow and ripen. Decorate me
with heavenly beauty. Let my entire life be
glorified through your grace.

X

Merciful God, let my life ceaselessly bear fruit.
Let it never turn into drought. Let me
always produce a harvest, even in times of
disappointment and sorrow. Grant that my
mistakes will turn into a blessing to me, and
that in my burdens and grief I may honor you.

XI

O God my Father, let me hunger and thirst
after you. Whenever I lag in prayer, fill my
soul with holy longings. Give me your peace.
Grant me your happiness.

XII

Merciful God, let your creation proclaim your
glory to me. Let the beauty of nature
fill me with love and honor. May the beautiful
glory of heaven point and pull me toward
my wonderful teacher.

XIII

My Lord and Master, anoint my lips so that
my speech will be gentle and full of love, so
that my brothers and sisters in
Christ are strengthened.

XIV

Almighty God, I thank you for the gift of
communion with you. Speak to me when I do
not speak to you. Come to me when I am far
from you and let me feel your grace when I
do not anticipate it. Grant that I may at all
times be awake to you.

XV

My Father, let sinners find peace in you. Let
heavy hearts come to rest. Strengthen the
tired and heavy laden through your power.
Let me also take part in your gifts.

XVI

Heavenly Father, help me to know your will
also in the small things of daily life and give
that I may be faithful to you. Help me to
seek your honor even when my task seems
unimportant. Make me faithful in doing
small things.

XVII

Merciful Father, I pray for all those whose
sins seem stronger than grace. May they
understand that Christ is greater than the
devil and that he has all the power.

XVIII

Holy God, I pray that my conscience may
become more sensitive. Deliver me from the
small sins which I tend not to count and
which often disturb the communion with you.
Cleanse me of my hidden straying.

XIX

Heavenly Father, I beg of you that the secrets
of your peace may enter into my heart.
Deliver me from all the distraction that
endangers me spiritually. Make me still in
your presence. Give me the water of life.

XX

O God, give that every day and every moment
may praise you. Let that be the most
beautiful day when it brings the most fruit,
the fruit of goodness, honesty and truth.

XXI

My God and Father, help me to believe that
you have the power to fully save. Deliver me
from the slavery of my evil habits. Give me
the freedom and the joy of your saints. Let
me joyfully travel the road of justice. Let my
soul find happiness in the Lord.

XXII

Merciful God, I pray for all those who are sick. Remember their sufferings and trials. Make me tender hearted and compassionate, so that I may serve them in your name. Make me a child who brings consolation.

XXIII

My Father, I thank you for the rising of the sun as eternity comes closer. The long night is passing. The sorrow will stop and the tears which have been shed in the dark valley will shine as the dew by the rising of the sun.

XXIV

Merciful God, let my heart give a perfect sound that it may give praise to you. Save my life from the sounds of grumbling and complaining. Let your grace become glorious in me so that my lips may sing your praise.

XXV

My Savior, point me your way. Stay close to me, instruct me, and teach me how I may live a Christian life. Help me to keep my eyes focused on you. Make me a good student of you.

XXVI

My Father, make me ready for today. Give that I will not be frightened, make my faith steady. Let me be still in the Lord and may I wait for him with patience.

XXVII

Merciful Savior, may the fountains of people's mercy bring refreshment and comfort. Take away the lovelessness which stands as a wall between people. Let your Kingdom come. Let my eyes see something of the holy brotherly love which you made possible through your death on the cross.

XXVIII

Merciful God, think about me in the labor of this day. Whenever it is your will, may I be successful and may I not do anything half way. Give that I through my work give praise to you and be a blessing to others.

XXIX

My Lord and Savior, grant me your peace. You know how quickly fear takes hold of me, how every danger frightens me. Let me remain peaceful in the storm and quiet during disappointments. I will eagerly believe and not fear, come and help me in my weakness.

XXX

Almighty God, let me ask and yearn for
your will. The resources of my strength
rest in you.Grant that I will not seek
broken vessels which hold no water.
Let me stay focused and bound
with you, then my soul will rejoice
in your abundance.

XXXI

Merciful Father, eagerly I want to
think of those who have grief and afflictions.
Give that I may have the right compassion.
Be there with your comfort for all those
who are sick. Let them feel the healing
power of your presence. Take pity on
all who feel dejected. Help them to
keep the faith.

September

I

Eternal God, may it be that today my faith
will bear fruit. Equip me with overwhelming
strength that my brothers and sisters may
also share. Grant me the spirit of self-denial
so that I may be willing, when it is your will,
to suffer for others. May I walk as a servant
child of the most high.

II

Merciful Father, bless the daily work of all
people that it may bear fruit to your honor.
Grant that we not become mute or unfeeling
beneath our burdens but become better and
more compassionate. Let us in our own
ordinary work, whatever it is, be as reverent
as if in prayer.

III

Heavenly Father, let your light accompany me
through all the unrest of life. Let me see my
earthly journey in that light. Grant that this
may be a light for me on the mountains and
in the valleys, in happiness and in adversity.
O my heavenly light, grant me your glow.

IV

My Father, be with me wherever I go.
Wherever difficult roads lie open for me and
where I am not sure of my way, point me to
the road of life and help me to walk it.

V

My Father, make me free from all bitterness.
When on this day an unpleasant mood should
threaten me, drive it away through the sun of
your love. Let all the trifles and bitterness
melt away in the glow of pure heavenly love.

VI

My Father, I will pray today for those whom I so easily forget. I pray for all those whom I do not love. Protect me from my own feelings. Bless my inclinations. Make me merciful. Grant me a clean heart that knows and seeks your likeness.

VII

My Lord and Savior, fountain of all light, also shine your light over me. Make me a child of the light. Let me walk in the light as you are the light.

VIII

Lord God, my heavenly Father, the work load awaits me and I do not know what concerns or what blessings lie ahead. Grant that I might begin with you and let me not stray from your unfamiliar road. Let me be comforted and happy trying to do your will.

IX

Merciful Lord, you have promised the people your peace. Help me that also I may know you. Grant that I will not find comfort in the world but that I may long for you. Grant me your peace which passes all understanding.

X

O Lord my God, I have a hunger for you, the bread of life. Awake in me a holy longing for your heavenly gifts. Whenever I hold back, ignite within me a new longing. Let me live for righteousness and let me not remain in my sins.

XI

Father of all mercies, let me never forget that I am a child of grace. Let the assurances of your love stay alive in me. May I experience your closeness as I await your return.

XII

Almighty God, strengthen my faith, my hope and my love. Let me not walk your road without hope but with steadfast step. Grant that I belong to those who know their calling, keeping the goal before their eyes, and loving the appearance of their Master.

XIII

My Father, grant me the mind of Christ. Take all my trivial and self-centered thoughts away and make my heart wide and full of love so that my brothers and sisters may live there.

XIV

My Father, grant me the power to be patient. Deliver me from irritability. Spare me from sharp, unkind words and all self-centeredness and lovelessness. Help me to serve my brothers and sisters without thinking about myself.

XV

My Father, let me walk in your light. When I fail to keep my eyes on you, I get lost and I sin. Help me to see you so that I may love you. Do not withdraw me from your face of grace.

XVI

Eternal God, I give you praise. Your road goes through deep waters, but your righteousness stands firm as the mountains of God. I thank you that I am assured of your faithfulness even when I do not feel it. Even the dark cloud is only the coat of your grace.

XVII

My Father, look in mercy at my past life. Forgive me for broken promises, my sluggishness in your service, and the scanty longings in me for truth. My sins give me pain. Help me that I may follow my Lord anew.

XVIII

Loving Lord, I thank you for the children who are around me. I thank you for the happiness they bring in this burdensome and difficult life. I thank you for sunshine which so often falls on tired and sad hearts. Let my heart through them remain young and happy.

XIX

Eternal God, illumine my eyes through your truth. Let me see all things in your light. Spare me from temptation and wrong doing. Grant me the mind of Christ.

XX

Holy God, may I know the true happiness. May I not fall to pride in this world. Grant that I regard holiness as worth more than gold. Grant that I may go after the eternal goods until I have received them.

XXI

Heavenly Father, grant me strength for the
task of this day. I thank you that I do not
need to ask in vain. Equip me for my duty
with strength and grace. Let me believe
in you with all my heart. Let me walk in holy
trust and bear fruit.

XXII

Holy Father, let me work today for you.
Let me know that you come to me in my
happiness and in my pain, in sunshine and in
darkness, in rest and in work.

XXIII

Merciful God, I praise you faithfully
and you love me without stopping.
Forgive my indifference and lukewarmness.
Renew your covenant with me. Make me
to stand fast and be sincere.

XXIV

Merciful Father, teach your children the secret of true growth in Christ, your dear Son. Spare us from seeking after the flesh, pride, and self. Make us children of peace. Grant us the spiritual power of a firm belief in you.

XXV

My Father, help me today so that in my appointed duties, conduct, and events of daily life I may hear your voice.

XXVI

Heavenly Father, help me today to become informed about the true spiritual life. Forgive all my mistakes and indifference. Grant me strength and steadfastness so that I through you may be strengthened and carried and rise to the heights of a hallowed life.

XXVII

Eternal God, let your grace unleash in my soul a wellspring of dedication to you. Deliver me from thinking primarily of myself, from being proud. Grant that there will be room in my thoughts for my brothers and sisters, and that in everything I may be a blessing to them.

XXVIII

My heavenly Father, help me that in every hour of this day I may stay connected to you. Bless every opportunity which appears in my life. Place also the least important in the light of your presence so that nothing will stay in the dark.

XXIX

My Father, give that as often as I must flee from the tempter, I will find refuge in you. Whenever it becomes a battle with temptation, grant me the power to withstand.

<u>XXX</u>

Heavenly Father, help me that I may lift my eyes to the mountains. Let me always come closer to you as my days continue. Let me look at your beauty and may that become my strength. Allow me to look from afar at the promised land.

October

I

Heavenly Father, let me look to you and become an image bearer. Let me in faith take part in your abundance. Make me clean in Christ Jesus. Let me show through my walk that I am the property of the almighty God.

II

Eternal God, grant me the strength I need for my daily task so I may not begin it in weakness but in the power of the living God. Give that I may rejoice in your help and trust therein so that my entire life becomes a song of praise.

III

O God of all power, renew the world through your Holy Spirit. Take away all pride and discord from our hearts. Make the people inclined to love their brothers and sisters. Let us become one through our faith in Christ.

IV

Eternal God, let your Holy Spirit enter into
my heart. May your Spirit stand by me in
whatever I do. His will controls my life.

V

Almighty God, we love and praise your holy
name. You give us the hope of eternal life.
I thank you that this light has been allowed to
fall upon my earthly journey. I want to
rejoice that I am not only dust of dust but
that a Godly life is within me. Let me never
forget why you called me.

VI

Eternal God, awaken in me a hunger and
thirst for righteousness. Grant that I not
aim too low in my life. May what is only
temporary not consume me. Let my heart
thirst after fresh water,the holiness found
in the fountains of life.

VII

Almighty God, make me always honest
in my duties. Fill me with the spirit of
love for then my burden will be light.
Let us see our work in your light so that
it may be blessed.

VIII

My Father, protect my heart from all
the pollution of the world. Wash me so that
I may become clean and my clothing
become white. Bless me so that I may live
a more holy life for you.

IX

My Lord Jesus, you are the light of the
world. Help me to walk in the light so
that I may yield heavenly fruit. Make me
a child of the light.

X

Heavenly Father, may I be a worthy
part of your family. Give that I may regard
everything a loss in order to win Christ
and be one in Him. Fill my soul with holy
respect and cause my feet to follow the way
of your commandments.

XI

My Savior, teach me to carry the cross. Help
me that I will not cast off my yoke in selfish
impatience. Let me not be sluggish today but
be awake and full of hope.

XII

My loving Lord, help me to be kind. I so often
treat the wounds of people roughly so that it
becomes even more difficult for them. Give me
the right compassion so that I feel the pain and
the disappointments of my brothers and sisters
and touch them with the sweetness of Christ.

XIII

Merciful God, bend my heart to your law.
Deliver me from my evil desires. Let me run
after what is true and holy. May I hunger
after your justice. Help me, most holy God.

XIV

Merciful God, rule my life's journey today.
Protect me from taking the first steps on the
wrong path. May it be that I seek not the
happiness of this world but walk in the
footsteps of my Savior.

XV

Almighty God, help me so that no power of
the enemy may darken your light in me.
Prevent earthly worries. Let your people feel
everywhere in life the quickening rays of
your grace, O Sun of righteousness.

XVI

My Father, make my thoughts pure at the
beginning of the new day. Take away
everything that is impure in me. Direct my
eyes to the heights of your mountain.
Let my entire life be ascension to heaven.

XVII

Strong and mighty God, look on my
weakness. Infuse my powerless heart with the
force of your power. Let me partake of your
strength. Let me win the battle.

XVIII

Father of love, I pray for all who are looking
for your road in darkness. Grant that they
may find you. Let them truly and longingly
do your will, so that their eyes will be
illuminated. Make them clean of heart, so
that they may behold you.

XIX

Eternal God, let me experience that I am
being overshadowed by your love and grace.
Surround and honor me in your goodness so
that I, without fear, may safely go forth
under your protection.

XX

O Lord, keep my words under your control.
Grant that my mouth will be a witness
for you. Cause my speech to be guided by
you. Through your spirit of grace govern my
association with others. Guard my tongue
which so often causes trouble. Make me a
true witness for you.

XXI

Eternal God, your grace is my hope and your
power is my strength. Grant that I find help
only through you. Let me accept you as my
Father through faith. Let my walk be
with Christ.

XXII

Holy Father, sanctify my entire being. Let my
hidden life be dedicated to you. Let my
most secret thoughts belong to you.

XXIII

Eternal God, I praise you. Your love reaches
as far as heaven is and includes all peoples.
Grant that I will keep your will before my
eyes. Your ever present mercy makes me at
peace in the assurance of your love.

XXIV

My Father may I show love toward others
and be kind. Make my heart open and
wide so that my brother and sister may find
room there. Grant that I may not put them
out of my thoughts but meet them with
compassion and love.

XXV

Holy God, let me live according to your will
today. Grant that my work will be performed
and dedicated to you. Help me to look upon
the Son of Man that I may please him in
my walk upon earth.

XXVI

My God and Father, let me hate what is
contrary to your Word. Grant that I not only
fear the punishment but abhor all sin. Grant
that sin may never charm me but will
always fill me with sadness.

XXVII

Lord, I know that in all things I can be
thankful for your grace. Let me never become
indifferent to your grace. Let me understand
that it is your goodness which daily and at all
times reaches out with eternal blessings.

XXVIII

Eternal God, grant me the spirit of mercy.
Deliver me from all that is unloving.
Make me tender and kind in your service
so that the beauty of one of your children
may also draw others in.

XXIX

Merciful God, grant me a new living
hope. Let me today expect great things
and believe in the gifts of your grace.
Let me see your wonders and discover
the evidence of your blessings.

XXX

Almighty God, bless me with power and peace. Let me do my daily work as one who is indebted to my Lord and Master. Grant that I work not out of compulsion but out of love for my God.

XXXI

Eternal God, your grace is my only hope. Without your goodness my life is dark. Let me abide in your love so that I may see your beauty. Grant me the spirit of obedience so that the secrets of my Lord dwell within me.

November

I

My Father, I place my trust in you this month. Make me understand how good it is to be able to trust in you. Let me taste your peace. Make my soul still in beholding the love of Christ.

II

Holy Father, let everything that is good and true re-echo in me. Whenever my life becomes dull make me alive again. Grant that I rejoice with those who rejoice and weep with those who weep. Let me stay connected to Christ.

III

Almighty God, renew my soul through your grace. Let me begin this day in your strength. Make me strong to do your will. Let me with a conquering faith today achieve my task.

IV

Great God, teach me to be gentle
of heart. Grant that I will not become
hard in prosperity or bitter in
disappointments. Help me to remain
tender-hearted and full of love.
Let me put my trust in you.

V

My Father, I thank you for all the
blessings which you have already granted me.
Keep my memory fresh so I will not forget
these good things. Let me acknowledge
that your mercy has always guided me
and let me praise your grace.

VI

My Father, I pray for the rejected and the lonely. Make my heart rich with compassion and love, so that I may seek the lost and point them to you. Help me to live in such a way that there will be those who, through my example and witness, will find the way back to my Father's house.

VII

My Father, drive away every thought which interferes with the bond of love I have with you. Open my heart and thoughts to your grace so that I may praise and love you every day.

VIII

O Lord my God, what do you expect from me today? Which task have you appointed for me today? Open my eyes so that I may know your will. Help me not to waste this day but let it be to me a day of eternal profit.

IX

Holy Spirit, bring my life to powerful growth. Let the wilderness in me blossom in love. When I stand alone in life without direction, may I become fruitful for Christ. Make everything new in me.

X

My Father, protect me today from the dangers of this world, save me from unbridled anger, from evil and greed. Save me from egoism and loneliness.

XI

Almighty God, let your love rest on my spirit and let my love rest in you. Grant that the cord which binds me to you does not tear. May I through all the unrest of this life remain connected to you in constant childlike obedience.

XII

My Father and my God, grant me the heart of a child. Make me dependent on your gifts. Let me never lose my reverence and admiration for you. Reveal to me every day your grace and bring me from glory to glory.

XIII

Heavenly Father, for you everything lies open. Look in mercy upon me and forgive what I have done wrong. Make me sincere so that I may confess my sins, hate them, and with determination turn away from them.

XIV

O my Lord, teach me to bear my cross without complaining. Spare me from being a bitter follower of you. Teach me the secret of joyfully continuing under a heavy load so that your power will help me in my weakness.

XV

Great and living God, grant me the only greatness that exists. Make me great by being humble and submissive, in being meek and faithful in loving you. Grant that I do not strive after worldly greatness but for the crown of eternal life.

XVI

My Lord and Savior, help me that I will today stay in communion with you. Let me partake in your strength and power, your joy, your rest, and your peace.

XVII

Father of all people, let me never
forget what the meaning is of your great
and holy name. When I call you Father,
I must love all your children. So often
I fall short in my love for all. Save me
from insincerity, and deliver me from all
unrighteousness in my prayers.

XVIII

Eternal God, may our feet follow the
way of your commandments. Help us to
serve you with greater diligence, so that
we not unwillingly take your road.
May we chase after the heavenly treasures
which you promised to all who persevere
in pursuing the crown.

XIX

Almighty God, spare my soul from all danger.
Grant that nothing may hurt me today, but
that everything will serve my welfare and that
even my enemies become a blessing to me.

XX

Eternal God, let me every day anew be
connected to you. May everything that I
desire and do meet your approval. The love
of Christ fills all my thoughts. Let all my
strength take root in you.

XXI

God of all mercy, show me the riches of your
love. Deliver me from all self-interest and
egoism. Make room in my life for all my
brothers and sisters. Let many tired pilgrim
travelers find refreshment and
comfort with me.

XXII

Eternal God, we live by your grace. I pray you,
make my soul wide and rich. Spare me from
self-sufficiency and vain satisfaction with
myself. Fill my heart with holy longing. Let me
not be satisfied until I awaken in your image.

XXIII

Eternal God, teach me how to worship you.
Grant that my soul will bow before you
in deep reverence. Let me discover your
closeness and fill me with holy reverence in
your presence. Teach me how to pray.

XXIV

Merciful Savior, clean my soul through your
holy Word. Drive away all thoughts that go
against you. Make my heart a temple unto life
and peace. Let your precious blood be
my only plea in life and in death.

XXV

My Father, control all of my days.
Help me so that I begin them with your
will and with trust in you and conclude
them in your forgiving grace. Let your
light shine over my life to the end.

XXVI

O Spirit of mercy, grant that I
never despise nor forget you. O that
I never make a decision without asking
you for wisdom and leading. I beg you
to illuminate my darkness and make me
more and more a child of the light.

XXVII

Heavenly Father, help me that I today without
interruption may gaze on you. Grant that
the bad and the low will not pull me down.
Help me to walk as a child of the Almighty
and all-powerful one who knows that his
citizenship is secure in heaven.

XXVIII

My Father, let me hear your voice when
you speak to me and then respond gladly.
Grant that I willingly obey, even when you
call me to a heavy task. Help me to take up
my cross and follow you.

XXIX

My Father, deliver me from my secret sin.
Save me from evil and lust. Change my
thoughts and inclinations so that I desire
nothing outside of your will, and drink from
the well of your joy and be filled.

<u>XXX</u>

My Father, I thank you for all who
have already entered your rest. Grant that the
sure hope of my heavenly inheritance shines
through as I do my daily tasks and glorify
you. Let me in my work build you
an altar and let everything that I do be a
pleasing sacrifice to you.

December

I

My Savior, grant me the grace of conviction
and may I ever inwardly stay connected to
you. Spare me from every thought which goes
against you. Make me a child of the light.

II

Eternal God, look down upon me in
mercy and let your pity in me unlock a
well of compassion. Let me reflect the
image of my Master. His love fills my life
and his sacrifice makes me willing to give
myself for others.

III

Father of all mercy, comfort me so that I may
comfort others. Grant that I may guard all
your hidden treasures and not keep your gifts
of mercy for myself. Let me use your
blessings joyfully so that my brothers and
sisters may receive a portion of them.

IV

Heavenly Father, make me weak as
I am to be strong in your grace.
Grant that I today in every way can fulfill
my life's task and do it with gladness.
Let me overcome every
temptation from the evil one through
him who has loved me.

V

Eternal God, in your light I can
move about safely. Let me not become
a victim of self-will and choose to stay
in darkness. Grant that I may hunger
after your Word and be led through
your Word.

VI

My Father, may it be that every
disappointment which I experience will
be a blessing to me. Let me also in my
defeats remain calm and continue
my trust in you. Let all my calamities serve
to increase your praise.

VII

Holy Spirit, awaken my dying strength to
new life. Inspire my heart with new promise.
Let my faith not wither in the bud
but ripen and bear fruit.

VIII

My Father, direct me to the right path
so that also in the most common
things I see you and in every situation
recognize your will.

IX

My Father, from you comes the fountain of life. Whenever I forget this my soul becomes barren and dry. Make my soul ever again alive through your power. Grant that I will ever again go to the fountain and drink the water of life. Savior, give me to drink.

X

My Father, govern my desires and subdue them to your will. Grant that they may bow in reverence for your purposes and never in presumptuousness go against you.

XI

O my Father in heaven, let me become like the children. Save me from pride and foolish over-estimations of self. Grant that I never will be ashamed to lean on you and daily beg at the door of your temple.

XII

Eternal God, your goodness is my life.
Let me today walk in the light of your grace
so that I will be filled with your comfort
and be a child of the light.

XIII

O God, rich in mercy, I pray for those who are
lost, who wander far from you. Father,
have mercy on those who have been rejected
among the people. Make many ready to
meet them with help and lead the distressed
to your Father heart. Turn their faces to
your light. Cleanse them from their sins.

XIV

Great God, grant that I not become afraid of
what this day might bring me. Be my refuge
so that I, as I await in peace, may have a
cheerful and confident faith.

XV

Eternal God, teach me to know Christ truly.
Let me not be taken over by my own
foolishness. You know the narrow borders of
my weakness. Let the Godly light shine in my
soul and make me strong in Jesus Christ.

XVI

Heavenly Father, help me to understand
why you have brought so much difficulty
in my life. Let me see that the pain and
trials are my friend. Grant that also my
disappointments may be a blessing to me.

XVII

Almighty God, lift my life to the light above.
Grant that I not choose human calculation as
a rule of conduct but follow your
commandments willingly and cheerfully.
Grant me a positive spirit and help me to speak
out for your truth wherever I may find myself.

XVIII

O Holy Spirit, may the spirit of mercy
be poured out over all the people.
May there be freedom from fear and error
and direct the people's hearts to the road
of light and truth. Let us all in our souls
experience the work of your grace.

XIX

My Father, take me anew into your
communion. Save me from indifference
and superficial worship. Let me through the
conquering power of your love be connected
to you steadfastly and closely.

XX

Merciful Father, you know my sins. Help me
to hate them. I yield to you the sins which
I love. Help me to conquer them. Grant that I
pay attention only to what is good and
seek after what is pure and clean.

XXI

God of all grace, let your Holy Spirit work on me and enter into the deepest hiding places of my soul. Grant that I keep nothing for myself but give my life over completely to you. Search my heart and thoughts and make me completely your possession.

XXII

My Father, let me learn from my mistakes and let it serve me as a warning. Through your grace let the foolishness of yesterday make me wise today.

XXIII

Great God, save me so that I do not think of you in small terms. Let your love and holiness truly become great in my life, then I will be rich and holy.

XXIV

My Father, I thank you that I may see your
face in Jesus Christ. Help me to love your
appearance. Let me pay attention to your
footsteps and to recognize them everywhere
when you come near me.

XXV

Lord Jesus Christ, my dear Savior, this is your
birthday. Let me honor and praise you.
Show me how I have to appear before you.
Grant me the spirit of reverence so that
I may see the secret of your glory. Let today
be a feast day for my soul.

XXVI

Almighty God, Lord of all spirits,
let us see you clearly in the face of Jesus
Christ whose birth we celebrate.
Give us a lively awareness of your presence
so that we may rejoice in you.

XXVII

Father of all mercy, let the light of your face shine upon us. Grant that I walk in your light so that it begins in me a pure and steadfast faith. Fill my heart with love for your truth.

XXVIII

King of honor, Lord of everything that is beautiful, grant me an open eye for what is heavenly and eternal life. Let me recognize where things are going badly in my earthly life. Point my eyes to that which is above. Make me a child of eternity.

XXIX

My risen Lord and Savior, let me taste your peace. I am so easily discouraged and frightened and I so long after rest, for lasting rest. Grant me your peace. Help me to trust you for time and for eternity.

XXX

Almighty God, your power is my protection.
I trust in you as I battle against the world,
flesh, and the devil. Come with your power to
help overcome my weakness.

XXXI

Heavenly Father, let this passing year be
commended to your love and grace. Turn all
that is evil to what is good, and forgive all my
sins. I praise and thank you for every victory
that this year brought me, but grant me a
humble spirit so that I expect nothing from
myself but everything from you. Grant that I
may finish this year in your peace.